10.00

92
EDI

Sabin, Louis
    Thomas Alva
Edison, young
inventor.

Thomas Alva Edison

YOUNG INVENTOR

Thomas Alva Edison

YOUNG INVENTOR

92
EDI

by Louis Sabin
illustrated by George Ulrich

Troll Associates

Library of Congress Cataloging in Publication Data

Sabin, Louis.
    Thomas Alva Edison, young inventor.

    Summary: A biography, focusing on the early
years, of the young man whose many inventions have changed
the lives of millions of people.
    1. Edison, Thomas A. (Thomas Alva), 1847-1931
—Biography—Juvenile literature.   2. Inventors—
United States—Biography—Juvenile literature.
[1. Edison, Thomas A. (Thomas Alva), 1847-1931.
2. Inventors]   I. Ulrich, George, ill.   II. Title.
TK140.E3S24   1983   621.3'092'4   [B]   [92]   82-15889
ISBN 0-89375-841-8
ISBN 0-89375-842-6 (pbk.)

Thomas Alva Edison

YOUNG INVENTOR

It was a warm spring afternoon. The brown-haired little boy sat on the ground near the barn. He liked watching the farm animals. There were chickens, pigs, horses, a couple of cows, and a flock of geese. One of the geese had caught the boy's attention. Three-year-old Thomas Alva Edison intently watched the bird.

The goose was sitting on three eggs nestled in a pile of straw. Sometimes she got off the eggs, turned them a little, then sat down again. The little boy wanted to know why the goose did that. So he watched and waited to see what would happen.

"Peep-peep! Peep-peep!"

The goose moved off the eggs. They didn't look the same anymore. One was cracked in half. A tiny, down-covered head stuck out. Another egg was just beginning to crack open.

"A baby goose!" the little boy cried out. "That's what the big goose was doing!"

Al—the name everybody called him—thought about the way the egg had hatched for a long time. It was the most exciting thing he had ever seen.

The next morning, Al ran out to the barn without waiting for breakfast. He picked up a large handful of straw and shaped it into a nest. Then he went into the hen house and came out with two eggs. He put them in his nest and carefully sat down on them.

9

Time passed. Al got up and turned his eggs the way the goose had turned her eggs. He sat down again. After a while his father came into the barn. "What are you doing, Al?" Samuel Edison asked.

"Hatching chickens," the little boy answered.

Mr. Edison scratched his head and smiled. "Sorry, son," he said. "I'm afraid it won't work."

"Why not, Papa?" the boy asked.

Mr. Edison explained that only a hen could hatch chicken eggs. She knew just how warm to keep them, and just when to turn each one. It was something people couldn't do. Still, Al's father told himself, it was pretty good thinking for a three-year-old—and just like Al to come up with an idea like that!

The young Edison boy wanted to know about everything around him. He looked and listened and asked countless questions. He wandered freely over the family's farm, sat at the edge of the local canal, and examined every last item in the general store. To young Thomas Alva Edison, born on February 11, 1847, in Milan, Ohio, his home town was a wonderful place.

Milan was a busy little town. Farmers from all over the state brought their crops to Milan because it was close to Lake Erie. Then dock workers loaded these crops onto ships that went up the canal into the lake. From there the ships went to big cities like Cleveland and Buffalo.

Milan was also a stopping-off place for wagon trains heading west. There was a steady march of wagons, especially after gold was discovered in California in 1849. Little Al liked to talk to the

travelers. He wanted to know where they were coming from and where they were going—and why, and whether they had seen Indians or had had any great adventures. He wanted to know *everything!*

Mr. and Mrs. Edison never stopped Al from doing anything, so long as it was safe. Al was the youngest of the Edisons' seven children. And the whole family enjoyed the little boy's clever remarks. Everyone gave him lots of attention.

Suddenly, it seemed, things began to change in Milan. Business was slow, stores were closing, and the canals had no ships on them. This was because a railroad had just been built through Ohio. Now the farmers shipped their crops by train. They didn't need the canal, and they had no reason to come to Milan. The busy little town was busy no more.

So, in 1854, when Al was seven, the Edisons moved to Port Huron, Michigan. It was a large, booming town right on Lake Huron and only a few miles from Canada. Here Mr. Edison did well. He ran a lumber business, sold grain and feed for animals, and grew crops on his small farm.

Al had his first taste of school in Port Huron. The school was run by the Reverend G. B. Engle, a very strict teacher. Mr. Engle didn't let the students ask any questions. They had to learn their lessons by heart and recite them on command. The rest of the time, they were ordered to sit straight-backed and silent. If they made any mistakes in their work, giggled, whispered, or

14

misbehaved, Mr. Engle punished them.

Al, so used to freedom, couldn't stand being in Mr. Engle's school. He sometimes daydreamed or wriggled in his seat or kicked the back of the chair in front of him. Each time he did, Mr. Engle was sure to catch him.

After a few weeks of this, Al ran away from school and refused to go back. His mother wanted to know why. He told her how horrible each day had been, and how scared he was every minute. Mrs. Edison was furious at Mr. Engle. That was no way to run a school! She had been a teacher herself. She knew that children didn't learn by being beaten and frightened.

"You are not going back to that place," Mrs. Edison told her son. "I'll make up lessons for you at home. This will be your school, and I will be your teacher. I promise you'll learn more—and a lot faster—my way."

Mrs. Edison had another good reason for keeping Al out of school. Ever since he was a baby, Al had gotten sick every winter. He would catch cold, develop a heavy cough, and get serious ear infections. And each winter he suffered from earaches and sometimes could not hear well. In fact, in later years, Edison's hearing got worse and worse, until he became almost totally deaf.

Young Al enjoyed his new "school" very much. Mrs. Edison had a simple way of teaching. She gave Al books to read. Then they talked about what he had read. By the time he was nine years old, Al had gone through *Parker's Natural and Experimental Philosophy* (a beginner's science book), two novels by Sir Walter Scott—*Ivanhoe* and *Rob Roy, The Penny Encyclopedia,* Sears's *History of the World,* and many other books of fact and fiction.

Young Edison was a very fast reader. He enjoyed his mother's praise for finishing each book so quickly. And there was another reward. Mr. Edison gave Al a quarter for each book the boy read and understood.

Al's mother also gave him lessons in arithmetic, geography, and penmanship. He was a fine pupil when it came to geography and penmanship. He had good, clear handwriting, and he could draw very nicely. The maps he made were as neat and well done as any printed map in a book.

But when it came to arithmetic, Al struggled. For the rest of his life, arithmetic remained a puzzle to Edison. When he later became an inventor, and the plans for one of his experiments needed some math to be done, he always asked one of his assistants to do it. Edison could imagine new and wonderful inventions. He could draw plans of the thing he imagined. And he could name and describe each part. But he always

turned to others when the plans needed work
with numbers.

There was another side to Al's education at
home. Mr. Edison was in charge of a lighthouse at
the edge of Lake Huron. Part of his job was to
take care of the fog whistle and the boiler that
gave the whistle power. Whenever Mr. Edison
had to oil or repair the engine, he took Al with
him.

The boy loved to help his father work on the two-horsepower engine. It had a large, turning cogwheel and a lever that opened a valve to let steam through the whistle. The force of the steam would make the whistle blow. Al never tired of watching how the cogwheel worked. And it's clear that he learned a lot, because the cogwheel played an important part in many of his early inventions.

Young Al also learned how to run a business. When he was nine years old, he and Michael Oates, a boy who did chores for Mr. Edison, sold vegetables. They gathered onions, cabbage, lettuce, peas, turnips, beets, potatoes, and carrots and loaded them on an open wagon. Then they hitched up a horse to the wagon and peddled the vegetables in nearby towns.

Al's business was a big success. People liked to buy vegetables from the farm, delivered right to their door. On most days, he brought the wagon home completely empty. And when his customers started asking him, "Do you have any fresh fruit?" Al had another idea. He went to farmers who had fruit for sale. Then he bought their apples, pears, peaches, and plums and sold them at a good profit.

The boys sold fruit and vegetables for three summers. And they did very well at it. In fact, in the last year of the business, when Al was eleven, he made a profit of over six hundred dollars. That was a lot of money in 1858! In those days, butter cost ten cents a pound, eggs were twelve cents a dozen, chickens cost ten cents each, and ducks were fifteen cents each.

The Edisons were proud of their son's hard work and good business sense. Many grownups didn't make so much money in a whole year! Al had paid for all the food he carried on the wagon, he had paid Michael for helping him, and he still came away with more than six hundred dollars. But what impressed his parents most was that Al turned over every penny of that money to them. It was, he said, for his share of the family expenses.

Al found time for other things besides business and reading. Every evening, after supper, he went down to the cellar. There he had set up a science laboratory. It wasn't much more than an old worktable, a few shelves, and some bottles and pans. But it was enough equipment for him to try all kinds of experiments.

Whenever Al had pocket money, he spent it on chemicals. Soon he had more than two hundred bottles filled with chemicals. Each one was labeled "Poison." Some of the chemicals weren't dangerous at all, but Al wanted to make sure that nobody touched anything in his laboratory.

Al taught himself chemistry from a science book that told how to do different experiments. He loved to mix the liquids and powders, and to see what happened with each new mixture. He was really pleased when his experiments came out just the way the book said they would.

Sometimes Al had an idea that didn't come from the book. Once, he decided to test a chemical called Seidlitz powder. This is a powder that fizzes when added to water and that people take when they have stomachaches. Al watched the way bubbles rose when the chemical was mixed with water. It made him think of the way a balloon rose into the air when it was filled with gas. He wondered what would happen if someone took a very large amount of Seidlitz powder in some water. Would that person lift off the ground and fly away?

At first, Al's business partner, Michael Oates, wasn't too keen on being the guinea pig. But Al wouldn't give up. "Science needs brave people," he told Michael. "People who aren't afraid to try

something new. You're not afraid, are you?"

"I'm not afraid," Michael said. "But are you sure it's safe?"

"Of course," Al answered, smiling. "Every one of my experiments has worked. This one will, too. Anyway, don't you want to be the first human being to fly?"

Michael liked that idea. "All right," he said. "Let's do it."

Al mixed a large dose of Seidlitz powder and water. It fizzed and bubbled, and Michael drank every last drop of it. Then the boys went outside and waited for Michael to lift off the ground. For a while nothing happened. Then Michael started to groan with pain. He had a terrible stomachache.

Michael's loud groans brought Mr. and Mrs. Edison running out of the house. They soon learned the cause of Michael's pain. "You were very foolish to swallow chemicals you know nothing about," Mr. Edison told Michael sternly. "That stomachache should teach you a lesson. I don't think you'll do anything like that again. As for you, Al, I'm going to teach you a lesson!"

Mr. Edison's lesson was a sound spanking. When it was done, Mrs. Edison told the young scientist to clear his junk out of the cellar. Al begged for another chance. He swore he'd never do another experiment on people, that he'd keep his laboratory locked, and that he'd stick to experiments that came out of books. Al's parents gave it a lot of thought, and finally they agreed.

At about this time, the Edisons sent Al to another school. This was no more successful than his stay at Mr. Engle's school. Sometimes Al could hear what his teacher was saying, sometimes he couldn't because of his hearing problem. But the teacher didn't understand this. She thought he wasn't paying attention when he asked her to repeat something.

His fast reading also caused problems. While the other students were still doing a reading assignment, Al squirmed in his seat, gazed all around the room, or tapped his feet in boredom.

As Mrs. Edison later recalled, "The boy's teacher said he was addled and not worth keeping in school any longer. She told us he would never make a scholar."

Al stopped going to school. But his mother told him not to worry about it. He was as bright as anyone. He would learn well wherever he was. And one day he'd show all of them how wrong they were!

Mrs. Edison's belief in him was important to young Al. As he later said, "My mother came out as my strong defender when the schoolteacher called me 'addled.' I determined right then that I would be worthy of her and show her that her confidence was not misplaced.

"She was always kind and sympathetic and never seemed to misunderstand or misjudge me. If it had not been for her faith in me...I should very likely never have become an inventor."

In 1859, right after Al turned twelve, he went to work. This would be unusual today, but in those days it was common. In the nineteenth century, most young people finished school and got a job before they were teenagers. What *was* unusual was what Al did to earn money.

There was a train that ran between Port Huron and Detroit, Michigan. The trip took three hours each way. Al was sure that the passengers would get hungry and bored in that time. Why not sell them newspapers, books, magazines, fruit, and candy? So he asked railroad officials for

permission to sell these goods on the train. They said yes, and he was in business.

Every morning, Al got up at six o'clock and filled two baskets with food, books, magazines, and newspapers. He got on the train at Port Huron at seven. For the next three hours he sold his goods up and down the aisles of the passenger cars.

When the train arrived in Detroit at ten o'clock, Al stored his baskets in the baggage car. Then he got off the train and hurried to the Detroit Public Library. There he sat and read science books for hours. And any time Al had some money to spare, he would go to a drug-supply company and buy chemicals. He needed them for the new experiments he was reading about.

The *Herald* reported local news from the towns along the railroad line. It also ran news of the war, which Al got from telegraphers at stops along the line. Pretty soon the paper was making a fine profit of forty-five dollars a month.

Al might have spent the rest of his life in the newspaper business except for two events. The first was the explosion of his rolling laboratory, which took the newspaper equipment with it. The second was the result of a good deed done by Al in August 1862.

Al was selling newspapers in the Mount Clemens train station when he saw a small child walking across the railroad tracks. A moment later, Al was horrified to see a freight train coming. He threw down his bundle of papers, ran, and pulled the child to safety. The train whizzed by so closely that it clipped the heel of Al's left shoe.

The little boy's father, James Mackenzie, was the Mount Clemens station telegrapher. He was so grateful to Al that he asked what he could do to repay him.

"I'd like to be a professional telegrapher," Al answered. "Would you teach me?"

Mackenzie said he would be delighted to do just that. Al hired a friend to sell his goods for him on the train from Mount Clemens to Detroit and back. That made it possible for Al to get off the train at Mount Clemens and study with Mr. Mackenzie every day. They worked together for three months straight. "By this time," Mr. Mackenzie remembered, "Al knew as much about telegraphy as I did."

Because it was wartime, the Union Army needed experienced telegraphers. Many answered the call. This made openings for beginners, like Al, to fill the civilian jobs. At fifteen, he went to work at the Port Huron telegraph office.

For the next few years, Al Edison worked as a telegrapher in cities and towns all over the United States and Canada. One of the moments he would always remember came on the night of April 14, 1865. He was on duty in Cincinnati, Ohio, when the news came through that President Lincoln had been shot. Al never forgot the icy chill he felt as he took the message coming over the wire.

During those years as a telegrapher, Edison began inventing things. One device he built was a mechanical vote recorder. Another was a machine that automatically took messages off a telegraph wire and printed them on a strip of paper. It was an instant success. And, as a result, Al decided to become a full-time inventor.

In the years that followed, Thomas Alva Edison created hundreds of inventions that changed the way the world lived. They include the electric light bulb and the phonograph. Every time Al invented something, he would record his creation with the U.S. Patent Office. Holding a "patent" on the invention meant Edison was recognized as the inventor; it also meant he was the only one who could produce the invention or profit from it. The U.S. Patent Office granted Al a total of 1,093 patents, more than any other person in history ever received. Among these were important inventions dealing with motion pictures, the telephone, the telegraph, cement making, electric railroads, the storage battery, electric-power plants, and many more.

Thomas Alva Edison devoted all of his adult life to science. Once he had made enough money to be free of worry, he built a huge laboratory in Menlo Park, New Jersey. Then he hired a team of scientists and gave them everything they needed to work. Their only job was to dream up new inventions.

This was an idea that had never been tried before—paying a scientist just to think up experiments and try them out. Edison's team was so successful that others began to copy his brilliant idea of scientific "dreamwork." Today, every large company and university in the world has a research department. And it all began with Edison's group in Menlo Park.

October 21, 1929, was the fiftieth anniversary of Edison's invention of the electric light. Two years later, after his death on October 18, 1931, these words were spoken at his funeral: "Picture an electric-lightless, an electric-powerless, a telephoneless, a motion-pictureless, a phonographless world, and a faint realization of his greatness dawns upon us. By taking Edison and his works *out* of the world, we gain the keenest appreciation of Edison *in* the world."

It was a fitting tribute to Thomas Alva Edison's unique genius.